REALLY REALLY BIG QUESTIONS
about Science

Copyright © Kingfisher 2014
Illustrations © Marc Aspinall 2014
www.thetreehousepress.co.uk

Published in the United States by Kingfisher,
175 Fifth Ave., New York, NY 10010
Kingfisher is an imprint of Macmillan Children's Books, London.
All rights reserved.

Distributed in the U.S. and Canada by Macmillan,175 Fifth Ave., New York, NY 10010

Library of Congress Cataloging-in-Publication data has been applied for.

Design: Amy McSimpson
Editor: Andrea Mills

ISBN 978-0-7534-7181-4

Kingfisher books are available for special promotions and premiums.
For details contact: Special Markets Department, Macmillan,
175 Fifth Ave., New York, NY 10010.

For more information, please visit www.kingfisherbooks.com

Printed in China

1 3 5 7 9 8 6 4 2
1TR/0414/WKT/UG/140WF

REALLY, REALLY BIG QUESTIONS

about Science

Written by

Holly Cave

Illustrated by

Marc Aspinall

CONTENTS

CHAPTER 3
THE WEIRD AND THE WONDERFUL

CHAPTER 4
BRIGHT IDEAS

CHAPTER 5
THE BIG, WIDE WORLD

INTRODUCTION

NEVER STOP QUESTIONING

This book is packed with questions about science. You might have guessed that from the cover.

Where does the Internet live?

What makes something funny?

Is there such a thing as forever?

You could describe science as everything that we know about the universe. Science can make a good guess at answering some of the questions in this book, but there are other questions that we still don't really have a clue about. And that's okay. Science changes all the time as we find out new things. It has itchy feet. It grows and evolves. It never stays still.

A lot of science involves looking at things and experimenting with them. Mixing two substances together in a test tube to see if they explode; trekking through the rainforest to find a frog with purple legs and bulging red eyes; making massive machines to study the smallest particles in the world—the list is endless.

But there's a huge chunk of science that has to happen before any of these things do.

First, someone has to have a really good question about how the world works. Start with the what, which, why, when, or where of something, and go from there. You don't have to be a scientist for this, but if your head is bursting with ideas that you want to find out about, then maybe you should become one!

Science is also about asking difficult questions about what we should do. Science isn't perfect. It can hurt people and animals and cause problems in the world around us that are hard to fix.

What I'm really trying to say is that science is a way of thinking about the world. There are questions that haven't even been asked yet. Many people can carry out experiments and test new ideas. The really tricky part—the part that will make you go down in history—is asking the right question. Are you up to the job?

1

LIFE AND LIVING THINGS

Life started 3.7 billion years ago—and hasn't it been a blast? In those billions of years, life has exploded into all sorts of weird and wonderful forms. From invisible bacteria that make your feet stink to glow-in-the-dark fish and bloodsucking vampire bats, life certainly has some surprises up its sleeve.

We've come a long way from boring single cells to walking, talking creatures that can think for ourselves and figure out how long ago life began. But there's still so much that we haven't gotten our heads around. How did the millions of creatures on our little planet get to be so mind-blowingly amazing? And where did they pop up from in the first place?

WHAT IS LIFE?

Life is a little bit like magic. It is full of wonders, but we're sure it can all be explained somehow. People have always tried to pin down the meaning of life but, unlike sandcastles, footballs, and televisions, life isn't a thing; it's a process—something that happens over time. It's hard to capture it in a photograph or in words.

So is fire alive? You wouldn't think so, but it grows, changes, and adapts, feeds on wood for energy, creates new baby fires as it spreads, and does a lot of things that living creatures do. Things start to get confusing.

That is why scientists have created a checklist to separate living things from nonliving things. Scientists say something is alive only if it can do a whole list of things, such as growing, gathering energy from food, responding and changing to the world around it, and making new versions of itself. When you go into detail, fire isn't made up of cells—the basic units of life—nor can it control where it moves, like animals and plants can. . . just imagine if it could!

BRAIN BURN!

Astrobiologists are looking for life on other planets, such as Mars. But could aliens be so different from life on Earth that no one would even recognize them as living things?

SO WHAT ISN'T ALIVE?

I'm guessing you'll agree that rocks, clothes, and vacuum cleaners aren't alive. However, some things are more difficult to classify. We can't quite decide if viruses—microscopic things that can cause illnesses such as measles and the flu—are alive or not. They're very good at replicating themselves, but they need help to do it. They can make new virus families only inside animal or plant cells. Does this mean viruses are alive some of the time?

And is it possible for some things to be less alive than others? A squashed squirrel that's been lying on the road for weeks is completely and utterly dead, no doubt about that. A freshly squashed squirrel is also dead, but little pieces of it—individual cells and tissues—will still be working. Although neither squirrel is alive, is the one that got squashed two weeks ago less alive than the one that got squashed today?

When it comes to deciding what's alive and what isn't, scientists have to draw a line somewhere between these two scenarios. Where would you draw your line?

HOW LONG AGO DID LIFE BEGIN ON EARTH?

Planet Earth was formed a truly mind-blowing 4.5 billion years ago, and scientists figure that life finally got going about 800 million years later.

These numbers are so big that they are difficult to imagine, so let's pretend that Earth is only one day old and was formed at this time yesterday. On this scale, the first thing that we could call life popped up about four hours after Earth formed, but it was only after another 20 hours that more complex animals started to appear in the oceans. Dinosaurs hit the scene after 23 hours and lasted for 45 minutes. And humans like you and me arrived in the final few seconds!

Do you think we'll do better than the dinosaurs and last longer than three-quarters of an hour?

WHY DID LIFE BEGIN?

Once there was nothing, and then there was something. But what started it all? Like many scientists, American Stanley Miller thought it was all basically luck. In a famous experiment in 1953, he tried to re-create early Earth.

Miller put water and three gases—methane, hydrogen, and ammonia—inside glass containers. By heating the water—as the Sun would have heated the ocean—he made miniature clouds and rain. He even fired sparks into the mixture to act as lightning. Within a couple of weeks, molecules called amino acids that exist in every living thing had formed, along with other organic molecules such as sugars and fats.

So maybe that's *how* life began. But what about *why* life began? That's a much tougher question. Is there a purpose to life, or did it just, well, happen? What do you think?

HOW WILL LIFE END?

Scientists studying stars similar to the Sun have realized that they only last a certain amount of time.

Scientists think that the Sun will keep going for about another five billion years. When it starts to run out of fuel, it'll get bigger and bigger, making it too hot for life to continue. Eventually, it will swallow up our tiny planet—game over for Earth. But don't panic just yet!

We can't predict what might happen in the next few million years. We might travel to other planets, or a more advanced version of life could take over and colonize the Moon. Will life continue elsewhere?

WHICH CAME FIRST: THE CHICKEN OR THE EGG?

This is an ancient puzzle that baffled philosophers for thousands of years and got Greek philosopher Aristotle scratching his head. He realized that an egg couldn't just appear out of thin air any more than a bird could one day produce an egg for the first time. It's not only chickens that lay eggs, though. Reptiles were laying eggs thousands of years before birds appeared on Earth. So if you bend the meaning of the question, then I guess the egg came first!

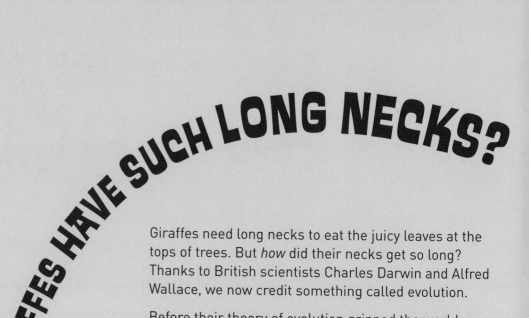

WHY DO GIRAFFES HAVE SUCH LONG NECKS?

Giraffes need long necks to eat the juicy leaves at the tops of trees. But *how* did their necks get so long? Thanks to British scientists Charles Darwin and Alfred Wallace, we now credit something called evolution.

Before their theory of evolution gripped the world, a French scientist named Jean-Baptiste Lamarck had a thought about giraffes. He figured that their long necks developed from spending time reaching for the treetops. His idea made sense: if giraffes spent years stretching, then perhaps they'd have longer-necked babies.

But Charles Darwin decided that species evolved because of *natural selection*—where only those best suited to the world around them live long enough to reproduce. Animals born with longer necks could eat more leaves when food got scarce, and they would live to pass on their long necks to their babies. Over thousands and thousands of years, giraffes as we know them today would have developed. That's the idea, anyway.

COULD ANIMALS HAVE BARCODES?

How many animals can you name? Ten, 20, or maybe 50? To date, scientists have found and named at least 1.2 million different kinds of animals. Each is known as a *species*. And, amazingly, we probably haven't yet identified most of this planet's species. The best guess is that there are about eight to ten million mystery life forms lurking out there somewhere.

Different species can look similar, but DNA barcoding might help us keep tabs on what's what. By finding a unique part of a species' DNA—the genetic "blueprint" inside its cells—scientists could give the creature a code. This is a little like the ones used to label food in grocery stores. Even using this new technology, it'll take scientists centuries to get the full list together.

DO DOLPHINS GOSSIP?

What would happen if you couldn't tell someone you were hungry or tired or that you felt sick? Living things *communicate* in order to survive.

When it comes to communication, humans are top dogs. We have written and spoken words, sign language, art, fancy codes and ways of instantly transmitting them around the world. Impressive when you think about it.

But some animals are good at communicating, too. Bees dance, plants make patterns, and dolphins really do gossip. Using a range of whistles and clicks, dolphins can let others know how they feel, and they seem to create a "name" for themselves. They also blow bubbles, move, and jump to communicate. Does this make them as intelligent as we are? What do *you* think?

CAN ANYONE INVENT A NEW CREATURE?

When it comes to making life, we know the ingredients, but we still have no idea how to bake the cake. The funny thing is that everything is made of the same basic ingredient—DNA. It's just organized in different ways.

American scientist Craig Venter has come the closest of anyone to making a new creature. He created a "synthetic cell" by creating a chain of DNA and inserting it into another cell to make a new kind of bacteria. He described it as "the first self-replicating species we've had on the planet whose parent is a computer." Its DNA even features an e-mail address that you can write to if you crack the code!

leaves green captures the Sun's energy, powering the production of sugars that feed the plant. If it weren't for this process—called *photosynthesis*—animals would never have lived, because there would not have been anything for them to eat. So the Sun plays a part all the way through our planet's food chain.

The heat and light from the Sun can take away life just as easily. Too much sunlight damages our fragile skin and can kill the plants and animals we need for food. The Aztecs of Mexico knew how important the right amount of sunlight is. They were so scared the Sun would stop rising every morning that they performed brutal human sacrifices to "feed" the Sun—cutting out people's hearts while they were still alive. Yikes!

BRAIN BURN!

Bringing deep-sea creatures to the surface kills them, so how will we ever learn what they are really like?

IS THERE ANYTHING AT THE BOTTOM OF THE SEA?

The deepest part of the ocean is called Challenger Deep, in the Mariana Trench. It can be found 7 mi. (11km) below the surface of the Pacific Ocean. It's deeper than Mount Everest—the tallest point on Earth—is high. Thousands have climbed Everest, but only a few people have ever gone to the deepest part of the ocean floor inside tiny submarines that can withstand the great pressure.

Even down there, life has been found. Marine biologists have spotted tiny creatures—shrimps, fish, and even weird organisms made of a single cell the size of your hand! Very odd when you think that your hand is made up of *millions* of cells.

In the dark depths, scientists have spotted fish with flashlightlike lights attached to their heads and teeth all over their tongues, plus scary "megamouth" sharks, bright red jellyfish, and eels with neon-colored skin. But we still know more about the surface of the planet Mars than we do about the bottom of the ocean. Want to go exploring?

2

AMAZING ME!

There are more than seven billion of us humans. Having evolved from much simpler organisms, we've ended up as top dogs in the great tree of life.

Maybe it's because we're so smart. Humans can make difficult decisions, create music, and even build spaceships to take us to the Moon. We might not be the fastest, the strongest, or the biggest, but we're definitely much more intelligent than many other creatures.

Not only that, but we're all different, with individual ideas and abilities that can change the world as we know it. So what makes you (yes, you!) so completely unique?

IS THERE ANYONE ELSE LIKE ME?

If you poked around inside the 10 trillion—that's 10,000,000,000,000—cells that form your body when it's fully grown, you'd find your DNA is one of a kind. DNA holds chemical instructions called *genes*, which tell your body what to do, affecting everything from your hair color to your personality.

Your genes help shape you. But every day of your life shapes you, too. It was only me who walked to the store this morning to buy a box of chocolate, petted a dog on the way home, and then chatted with my friend. No one else had that conversation with her—just me.

Everything you experience throughout your life, along with your genes, combine to make you the individual person you are. And you are certainly unique! There's no one else exactly like you in the world. There never has been, and there never will be.

WHY DON'T I LOOK LIKE A BANANA?

This seems like a stupid question. Why *would* you look like a banana? Well, scientists would be very quick to point out that because humans and bananas evolved from the same early organism, you share half their genes! Although they're slightly different, 50 percent of banana genes do the same job in your body.

And you might think that you look nothing like the old lady who lives at the end of your street, but in terms of our genes, all humans are 99.5 percent the same. It's just that 0.5 percent that makes you unique.

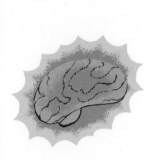

BRAIN BURN!

We share a gene with mice that gives them a tail. Luckily, our version of this gene is inactive! Can you imagine if it were active?

WOULD MY CLONE LOOK LIKE ME?

Identical twins share exactly the same genes. Do you know any? Can you tell them apart? It's usually possible. One may have a scar on their chin or have freckles or be thinner than the other. They're not exactly the same because they've had different lives. One might have hurt their chin falling off a bike, or one might sunbathe more or eat less than the other.

If scientists created a clone of you, then you would both have the same genes, so you would look the same—just like identical twins. However, if your clone grew up somewhere else, ate different foods, and got sick more often, you could both end up looking very different from each other.

WHAT MAKES YOUR BRAIN BETTER THAN A COMPUTER?

A computer can do a lot more than your brain, right? Like multiply 678 by 4,389 instantly, and accurately store thousands of details. So how could your spongy little brain—the size of both your fists pressed together—ever compete with this whizzy technology?

But it does. It lets you do everything from walking and talking to dreaming and drawing. The best brains have written beautiful music, painted masterpieces, and figured out why stars sparkle. And the brain's 100 billion cells (neurons) are always changing and growing, learning from every little thing that you do. Computers can't do that.

The human brain is the most complex thing in the world. It invented the computer. It never stops learning. It is also capable of emotion and imagination. It can even read and understand jumbled words—txet in wchih the ltetres all seem rodanm. A computer couldn't understand the jumbled words, but our mighty brains can. We still have so much to find out about the brain and how it works.

COULD I BECOME A MEMORY CHAMPION?

The neurons in your brain connect to one another to make a huge network, and every second, a million new connections are made. The more you do something—for example, swimming—the more connections are made and the stronger they get. By linking up, neurons lay down new memories so that you get better at swimming with more and more practice.

And practice makes perfect if you want to become a World Memory Champion, too. The best competitors can memorize the exact order of a pack of 52 playing cards in less than 30 seconds! Grab a pack and challenge your friends and family to a memory test—who can remember the most in one go?

ARE MY THOUGHTS PRIVATE?

Imagine you're tempted to push your friend into a swimming pool. She's fully dressed, the water's cold, and you just think how funny it would be for everyone watching. You look at your friend carefully. Does she know what you're thinking?

No one can "hear" your thoughts. They're silent words and feelings inside your brain. But sometimes you can give away what you're thinking. Your friend screams at the last second and ducks out of the way. She didn't *know* what you were thinking, but maybe you looked mischievous or she saw your eyes flick to the pool.

Scientists are getting pretty good at finding out what we're thinking. By looking at someone's brain in a machine called an MRI scanner, they can decide which emotion that person is feeling by checking the activity in their brain. And lie detectors monitor your heart rate, blood pressure, and other clues from your body to decide whether you're telling the truth. They can accurately determine whether someone's statement is true or false.

So with all these telltale signs to look out for, perhaps your thoughts aren't always as private as you believed they were! Now there's a thought. . .

"Laughter is the best medicine."

Author unknown

WHAT MAKES SOMETHING FUNNY?

WHY DO I ARGUE WITH MY BEST FRIEND?

It can be upsetting to fight with your best friend. But what if you were a robot and didn't have any feelings? Would that be better? You would never get annoyed or feel jealous. But you wouldn't be able to find something funny or feel love, either. Not having emotions doesn't sound so good now, does it?

We've evolved emotions to help us—they're in our genes. For example, fear helps us deal with danger, jealousy pushes us to be more competitive, and love makes us take care of each other. However useful some emotions are, others need to be kept in check. The anger that you feel when you argue with your best friend can be destructive. So the next time you have a disagreement, talk about how you're feeling instead of arguing about it.

Knock, knock.

Who's there?

Lettuce.

Lettuce who?

Lettuce in—it's cold out here!

Are you laughing? Sorry, my jokes aren't that good. But what *does* make you laugh? And what's the point of laughter anyway? Scientists think we developed laughter as a way of bonding with each other and overcoming our worries. Perhaps it was useful for calming down early humans after running away from another tribe or killing a buffalo. Funny things make everyone feel better.

Research shows that girls and boys tend to find different things funny, as do people from different countries. But no one knows exactly why I think my joke is hilarious and you might not.

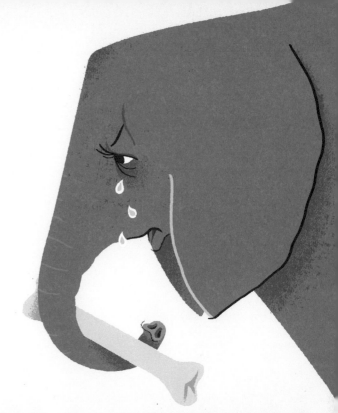

CAN ELEPHANTS CRY?

Are we the only creatures to have so many different emotions? An animal might *look* sad, but we don't really know for certain whether it is sad. And while some animals produce tears to clean their eyes, scientists don't think they cry because of sadness.

The elephant is one of the most intelligent animals around. They don't cry, but could they have feelings similar to ours? Some scientists think so. For one thing, elephants behave in certain ways when others die. They will often stay with the dead elephant for hours or days, stroking the body. They also visit the graves of dead elephants and pick up the bones with their trunks. To us, it looks like the elephants are upset and grieving. But are they *really*? How could we ever know for sure?

IS SOME SLEEP DEEPER THAN OTHERS?

Nodding off at night is one thing, but if you need an operation, then doctors might make you fall into a much deeper kind of sleep. Just some general anesthetic in your arm, then count backward from 10, 9, 8, 7. . . and you're out like a light. You can be prodded, poked, and cut open, and not only will you not feel a thing, you can't move and you won't wake up. Although doctors call it "putting you to sleep," it's very different from a normal nap.

General anesthetic was a great discovery because it means that people can have amazingly pain-free surgery. But here's the surprising thing: we don't know how it works! There's nothing to worry about because it's a very safe procedure, but does it matter if scientists don't understand why something happens? What do you think?

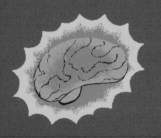

BRAIN BURN!

The longest anyone has gone without sleep is 11 days. He ended up hallucinating and unable to think straight!

WHY DO I DREAM ABOUT MY TEETH FALLING OUT?

You will spend about a third of your life asleep. As we sleep, our bodies go through different stages. . .

Dreaming is a different matter. I don't know about you, but I always dream about my teeth falling out. A famous Austrian psychologist named Sigmund Freud believed dreams were the hidden depths of our brains trying to figure out problems in our lives. Everyone has different ideas. Some people say I dream about losing my gnashers because I'm scared of getting old or I'm worrying about something.

Will we ever understand *why* we dream? Maybe dreams are just a way of keeping us asleep so that we rest properly, or maybe they're a roundabout way of helping us form memories about things we've learned during the day. Who knows? Zzzzz. . .

3

THE WEIRD AND THE WONDERFUL

There are a lot of things that happen on Earth that, at first glance, seem rather odd. Water falls out of the sky, eruptions release hot stuff, and strange patterns appear where we least expect them. How do glasses sing? And why don't electric eels ever electrocute themselves?

Everything in this chapter—flashes of lightning, spectacular sounds, and the perfect spiral of shells—is all completely natural thanks to the laws of physics that make our world so complex and so incredible. Scientists and mathematicians have cracked some of the hidden codes, but there's still much, much more to learn!

IS AIR JUST EMPTY SPACE?

Air might look as though there's nothing in it, but breathing oxygen keeps you alive, so oxygen must be all around you, right? Right. And oxygen's not the only thing in the air. Other gases, such as nitrogen and carbon dioxide are also in air, and so are tiny water particles.

Scientists once thought the smallest particles were *atoms* and believed they were the basic unit of everything. But in 1897, British scientist J. J. Thomson discovered the *electron*—a particle that's *part* of atoms. Since then, scientists have found that atoms are also made of other smaller particles called *protons* and

neutrons. And those particles are made up of even smaller particles called *quarks*!

Absolutely everything in the universe is made of unimaginably small particles that you can't see without a microscope. If the particles are tightly packed together, they make solid objects that you can see and touch. Air is transparent, or see-through, because its atoms are so far apart that you end up seeing nothing at all. But don't be fooled—just because you can't see them, it doesn't mean they aren't there!

CAN ANYTHING BE IN TWO

Imagine if you could be in two places at once. Just think where you could go. You could be riding a roller coaster *and* be in school, both at the same time!

Sadly, that's impossible. But if you were an electron, you could, in effect, be in more than one place at a time. How? Well, single particles, like electrons, behave very differently from you, me and other solid matter. They exist under their own crazy set of rules that scientists call *quantum mechanics*. As well as being a single particle, an electron also behaves like a wave. Buzzing around at superfast speeds, an electron's not just in two places at once; physicists say it's *everywhere* at once.

But if we're made of these tiny particles, then why aren't we in multiple places at once? We're still waiting for another big brain to come along and figure that out. . . Think you can help?

DO GHOSTS REALLY EXIST?

Ever had a spooky sense of being watched, or seen a strange shadow flit across a room? Then maybe you've seen a ghost. . .

Most scientists would say that ghosts are nonsense and are nothing more than your mind playing tricks on you. But ghost hunters spend hours wandering through "haunted" houses after dark, looking for the shadowy spirits of people long dead. And millions of people around the world claim they've seen one.

Some scientists have suggested that ghosts could be a glimpse into *parallel universes*—alternative realities that exist alongside our own universe but are normally hidden. Many physicists believe in parallel universes, but ghosts? That's another matter!

HOW CAN A GLASS

Take a deep breath, open your mouth wide, and try to hit the highest note you can with that beautiful voice of yours. *Laaaaaaaaa!* Now try to make a glass sing!

How? Here's the trick: ask to borrow a wine glass and hold it steady on a table by covering the base with your fingers. Dip your finger into some water and then rub it around the rim of the glass in a firm, steady movement. Ta-dah! The glass is singing!

The sound is caused by *vibration*. When you rub the glass, you make the particles in the glass vibrate. As they are vibrating, they make the air around them vibrate, too, creating waves of sound that travel to your ears. If you make the wine glass vibrate too much, it will shatter. You won't be able to do this just with your finger, but opera singers have been known to break glasses by singing the right note loudly enough!

SING?

HAVE YOU BEEN HERE BEFORE?

Have you ever had that strange feeling that you've been somewhere or done something before? Sometimes it lasts for only a few seconds, but whatever it is you're up to, you're sure it's already happened. Two-thirds of people get this funny sensation, and it's called *déjà vu*—French for "already seen."

Some scientists think that the sensation is a mistake coming from the memory-making part of your brain that tricks you into thinking the present has already happened. Others figure that your brain falsely links what you're seeing or doing to something very similar from the past and tells you it's the same thing. *Déjà vu* is a confusing idea, and it still has scientists puzzled.

Because it happens so rarely, it's hard to study. Scientists can't drag you into a lab, put you under a brain scanner, and just leave you there until you feel a sense of *déjà vu*—it might take years! So how will we ever be sure about what happens in the brain during this weird experience? That's one for you to mull over!

WHAT'S THE BIGGEST NUMBER IN THE WORLD?

Scientists are always telling us that the universe is infinite—that it goes on forever and ever without an end, or that it doesn't have an edge and wherever you went, you would eventually end up back where you started. If we don't know how big the universe is, then how can there be a biggest *anything*?

Mathematicians often use infinity (∞) in place of numbers in their calculations. But sometimes they need to put a limit on things. They need the biggest *meaningful* number, a digit that is huge but still useful for their calculations. That number is called Graham's number, after the American mathematician Ronald Graham, who first used it.

This whopper of a number is listed in the *Guinness Book of World Records* as the biggest number ever used in a math calculation. I'd write it down here for you if I could—but I can't. It's simply too big! It would take more pens, paper, and people than there are on Earth to write it down. What I can tell you is that it's a whole lot of 3s multiplied together A LOT of times. Is your head hurting yet?

340236474548882222161518340237018303718871783027178718302091825896753560430869938016892498892680995101690559199511950 ... 2029242108335082783 ... 3623493162912495443788874960628892117250630013

WHY DO SHELLS SPIRAL?

The world around us is full of patterns, from spiky snowflakes to hexagonal honeycombs made by busy bees.

This is what math is really about: finding patterns and making sense of what seems to be complete and utter chaos. Patterns can help scientists discover new things by showing them where to look—think of it like a giant puzzle with big pieces that need to be put together.

Spirals are found in a lot of places: in snail and seashells, in the seeds of sunflower heads, in molecules such as DNA, and in the shape of galaxies such as our own—the Milky Way. It's a pattern called the golden spiral. It may be that shells and other natural things grow in spirals because it allows the maximum possible growth within the smallest space. What do you think?

WHY DO THINGS EXPLODE?

One minute, everything's quiet and then, with just the strike of a match or a tiny spark. . . BOOM!

Long, long ago, our ancestors learned how to make fire. About 1,000 years ago, the Chinese created the first fireworks, and 150 years ago, the Swedish inventor Alfred Nobel came up with a formula for an exceptional explosive—dynamite.

But what makes things burn and explode? While early explosives were found by playing with different substances, chemists today can explain exactly why explosions happen and why things burn. It usually has to do with the same part of the air we breathe—oxygen. Particles from the substance combine with oxygen atoms in the air to create a *chemical reaction*. Energy is released in the form of heat and light. If this happens suddenly, it makes an explosion.

WHY DOESN'T AN ELECTRIC EEL ELECTROCUTE ITSELF?

Small amounts of electricity can be found all over the place. When you rub a woolen sweater against your head, static electricity makes your hair stick up. There's electricity inside your body, too. Your nerves transmit tiny pulses of it to make your muscles move and send messages to your brain. Even your heart beats thanks to electrical impulses.

Some animals are a little more creative with electricity. The electric eel catches food and protects itself by producing powerful electric shocks. Lurking in South American rivers, these funny fish store electricity in special cells that are like tiny batteries.

Scientists aren't sure why electric eels don't shock themselves, but the electricity is released from their tails—distanced from their vital organs. The current zaps straight through the eel's skin and into other nearby animals, so keep your eyes peeled if you're ever swimming in the Amazon River!

CAN LIGHTNING STRIKE TWICE?

Lightning is a kind of electricity that accumulates in clouds during storms. Thunder is the sound of the air expanding around the hot lightning bolt. You always see the lightning before you hear the thunder because light travels faster than sound.

Now, there's an old saying that lightning never strikes twice. If you live until you're 80, your chance of being struck by lightning is 1 in 10,000. So it's unlikely that you'll even get hit once. However, some people have pretty bad luck! American Roy Sullivan was hit by lightning seven times in his life. But Roy survived every single strike, so does that make him lucky or unlucky?

WHY CAN'T I JUMP LIKE A SUPERHERO?

Ever wondered why you can't spring like Spider-Man or bounce around like Batman? Like everything else, you fall back down to the ground again. That's because of something called *gravity*, and there's no getting rid of it.

In the 1500s, Italian physicist Galileo is said to have dropped balls of different weights from the Leaning Tower of Pisa to prove that everything, no matter what weight, hits the ground at the same time. Gravity affects everything in the same way, so if you and an elephant jumped from a plane at the same time, you'd hit the ground together.

In 1687, English physicist Isaac Newton published a mathematical formula for gravity, and 228 years later, German-born scientist Albert Einstein rewrote this formula as part of his theory of *general relativity*. Gravity is one of those things that everyone knows about, but scientists don't understand what causes it. That makes gravity one of the universe's biggest secrets. So we can say that you can't jump like a superhero *because* of gravity, but we can't yet explain *why*!

COULD AN ASTEROID DESTROY EARTH?

It's the stuff of Hollywood disaster movies, but Earth has been around for 4,500 million years, so it's doing pretty well so far! Luckily, our planet has a thick atmosphere around it—like a blanket—that protects us from space rocks such as asteroids, meteors, and comets. Every year, hundreds of space rocks burn up in our atmosphere before they reach the ground. If you've ever seen a shooting star, that was one of them.

But Earth hasn't escaped completely. In its history, space objects have caused massive damage. The extinction of most of the dinosaurs about 66 million years ago is thought by most scientists to have been caused by an asteroid crashing into Earth. The United States' space agency, NASA, scans space for objects that could pay Earth an unwelcome visit, so don't worry— we should spot trouble coming centuries in advance!

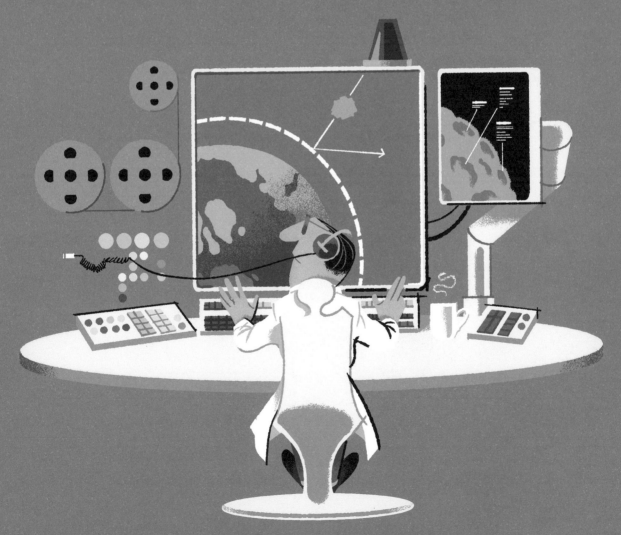

4
BRIGHT IDEAS

We're surrounded by incredible inventions that make our lives easier, healthier, and more enjoyable. They also give us fun things to do when we're bored. Some of the brainiest, most creative people who have ever lived are famous for conjuring up concepts and creating equipment that transformed our world completely. We owe a lot to them, from the airplane that takes us on vacation to the zipper that does up our jeans—and everything else in between.

Where do these scientists and inventors get their ideas from? Can some inventions be both good and bad? Where does the Internet live? Let's try to answer some of these questions now.

WHAT'S A "LIGHT BULB MOMENT"?

You're in a dark room and you hear a noise. It might be a mouse—eek! You turn on the light and you see it's only a branch rubbing against the window. Whew!

Turning the light on makes you see the world differently. When this happens inside your brain, we call it a "light bulb moment." Something confusing suddenly makes sense. It's as if a switch has been flicked between your ears and there's a flash of inspiration—wow!

But not all great inventors are inspired so suddenly. Funnily enough, American inventor Thomas Edison, creator of the world's first long-lasting, affordable light bulb (and a lot more besides), didn't have a light bulb moment. He just worked really hard. "I've not failed," Edison is believed to have said. "I've just found 10,000 ways that won't work!"

WHAT'S "WHEELY" THE BEST INVENTION?

Some modern inventions—things like spaceships, swanky smartphones, and brightly colored lasers—are amazing. They make you think, how on earth did someone invent that? Other things we just take for granted. There's nothing clever about sliced bread, balloons, or the wheel, *is there*?

Hold on a minute. Where would we be without the wheel? As simple as it seems, someone must have invented it. And judging from ancient drawings showing wheeled, horse-drawn wagons, scientists figure that the wheel started rolling 6,000 years ago!

The wheel's pretty useful, but is there such a thing as the *best* invention? Think about it. . . What's the one thing *you* couldn't live without?

CAN RADIATION COOK MY DINNER?

We use different kinds of *radiation*—waves of particles with a lot of energy—for plenty of stuff, such as treating illness, tracking planes through the sky, making radio broadcasts, and even cooking food!

One day in 1946, when American engineer Dr. Percy L. Spencer was working on some radar equipment, he realized that the candy bar in his pocket had become gooey. It wasn't warm in the laboratory, so what had melted it? He realized it must be the radiation coming from the radar machinery. The modern microwave oven was born from that accidental discovery!

So how does the microwave oven work? Well, water, fat, and other food particles absorb energy from the radiation inside microwave ovens. As the food particles gather energy, they move around and release heat to cook your dinner. Yummy!

IS THERE ONLY ONE WAY TO SOLVE A PROBLEM?

Scientists and engineers have invented all sorts of things, from bridges and unicycles to sunglasses for dogs. But could these inventions have been invented differently?

The television is a really clever invention. It's always been a way of watching moving images, but how it actually works is always changing.

John Logie Baird's early television set was mechanical—moving parts made it work. Shortly afterward, Philo Farnsworth made it electronic, and now, TVs are digital. A lot of other inventors from around the world have helped develop the modern television, and it's still changing.

If none of television's inventors had existed, would it be around today? Maybe we wouldn't have television at all, or maybe it would work differently.

WHERE DOES THE INTERNET LIVE?

Let's get techy. The Internet is a global network of computers. The World Wide Web is the collection of all the pages that you look at using the Internet, written in a computer "language" called HTML.

The Web's creator—British scientist Tim Berners-Lee—could have made a fortune from selling the use of the technology, but he chose not to. He thought it should be free for everyone to enjoy. The queen of England did give him a knighthood, which shows appreciation for his hard work.

The Internet is everywhere all at once, "living" in all of the computers and data storage centers connected to it, in the wireless signals, and in the cables that zigzag our planet beneath the oceans. Mind-blowing stuff.

COULD I CLIMB LIKE A GECKO?

Sometimes scientists are inspired by nature. They mimic (copy) natural things. This is called *biomimetics*.

Some scientists have looked at how geckos scale walls and cling to ceilings and wondered if humans could do this, too. They studied the lizard's toes under powerful microscopes and found out that thousands of tiny hairs help it "stick" to even the smoothest surfaces.

By copying nature, scientists have created a super material. Get your hands on it (literally), and you'll be able to scoot up the Empire State Building in New York!

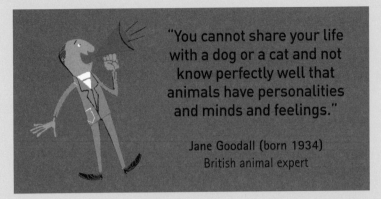

"You cannot share your life with a dog or a cat and not know perfectly well that animals have personalities and minds and feelings."

Jane Goodall (born 1934)
British animal expert

IS IT RIGHT TO TEST MEDICINE ON ANIMALS?

Any medicine or vaccine you've ever taken was tested on animals to make sure it works and that it's safe. But this is controversial. People have very different opinions about whether this is acceptable. Is it ethical or not?

It may not seem right that animals should suffer, but many scientists insist that animal testing is the only way we'll find cures. They say their labs are checked to make sure the animals experience as little pain or discomfort as possible. Some people think that it's acceptable to test on animals like mice but that we shouldn't use monkeys because they're more intelligent and are more aware of being caged. Monkeys might even have *feelings* like we do. So maybe it matters how brainy an animal is?

Safe treatments for diseases such as tuberculosis and diabetes were created by testing them on animals first. But just because a medicine works and seems safe for a mouse or a dog doesn't mean it will be all right for us. Medicines tested on animals can still react badly in the human body because we are very different from a mouse!

Would you take a medicine that you knew had been tested on animals, even if it was your only chance? Sometimes questions don't have a straightforward yes or no answer.

WHY AM I ALWAYS

Ever get sick of being ruled by time? Time to wake up, time to start school, time to eat dinner, bedtime. . .

We didn't invent time itself—there's always been a past, a present, and a future—but people have invented ways of *keeping track* of time. We started out with sundials and hourglasses, and now the best timekeepers are high-tech atomic clocks. The world's most accurate clock, used by scientists at the UK's National Physical Laboratory, loses or gains no more than a second in 138 million years! Now that's good timekeeping.

"The only reason for time is so that everything doesn't happen at once."

Albert Einstein (1879–1955)
German-born physicist

LATE FOR SCHOOL?

As much as we try to pin time down, scientist Albert Einstein figured out that time varies depending on where you are and how fast you're traveling. Crazily, clocks run at slightly different speeds in different parts of the world. So really, there's no such thing as "the time." Try telling that to your teacher next time you're late for school!

WHERE DO PLASTIC BOTTLES GO TO DIE?

Plastic isn't just used for bottles—it's all over the place. It's made from oil, the gooey black substance deep in the ground that also powers cars and is burned to make electricity for our homes.

How do we get rid of plastic once we've finished with it? Well, that's a big problem. We are making millions of plastic things, but they take thousands of years to break down and disappear. Earth is filling up with trash.

That's why we've started recycling. We can melt down some kinds of plastic and make it into new things. Scientists are coming up with a lot of other ideas for how we can reduce our waste, too. New plastics made from plants can break down naturally in the soil. Special bacteria munch on plastic, eating it out of our way!

BRAIN BURN!

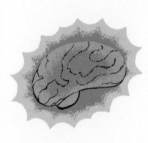

Offices with recycling containers use more paper than offices without, so would it be better for the environment if we just tried to use less paper?

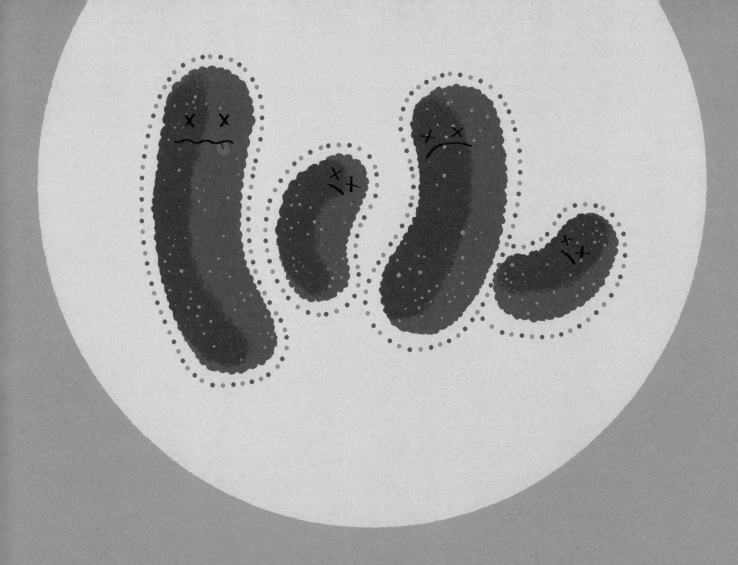

HOW DO WE KNOW THINGS EXIST IF WE CAN'T SEE THEM?

We've had a look at a lot of things in this book that you may never see for yourself. Viruses, bacteria, genes, and atoms, for example, are too tiny for you to see with your eyes only.

Scientists magnify these miniature things using microscopes. The most powerful microscopes create images using electrons—those little particles that are part of atoms and all matter. But scientists know they're

not quite seeing things in an electron microscope *as they really are*. For a start, the thing they're looking at has to be dead. So you can look at a virus, but you can't see it infecting cells or moving around. Plus, electron microscopes only show things in black and white and can also damage the actual thing you're trying to look at.

Is seeing believing? Can you believe something is real without ever seeing it for yourself?

5

THE BIG, WIDE WORLD

Where's your home? Your street, your country, your planet, and even your solar system are just the beginning of the story! There are billions of other stars and planets in our galaxy, and billions of galaxies in the universe. So what would an alien trillions of miles away, write on the envelope if it wanted to send you a letter?

Does the universe have an edge? Can you change the past? What else has scientists scratching their heads?

DOES THE UNIVERSE HAVE A BIRTHDAY PARTY?

Once upon a time, you didn't exist. Then one day you started growing inside your mom, and about nine months later out you came. Every year you celebrate your birthday with balloons, cake, and presents, if you're lucky! Scientists think that the universe must have a birthday, too, because about 13 billion years ago it just popped into existence. They give this "popping out" a grand name—they call it the *big bang*.

Your mom gave birth to you, but what gave birth to the universe? That's a much trickier question. We're eager to figure out where everything came from, but will we ever know for sure? Does it matter if we never know?

IS THERE SUCH A THING AS FOREVER?

If the universe had a start, does that mean it'll have an end? By looking at the stars, scientists can see that the universe is still expanding from the *big bang*. Everything's getting colder and farther apart. Many think that the universe might end when it gets as cold as possible. This chilling idea, or *theory*, is known as the *big freeze*.

Or maybe there'll be a *big rip* and the universe will tear apart, starting with solar systems, planets, and stars, and ending with the destruction of individual particles. Things might even go into reverse and it'll all end in a *big crunch* as the universe collapses into a black hole!

When the universe is gone, time will disappear, too. And if time can end, then forever is just a fairy tale. When the universe waves goodbye, what will be left? Nothing? Or will a new universe be born?

"I'm comfortable with the unknown. . . that's the point of science. I don't need answers to everything. . . I want to have answers to find."

Brian Cox (born 1968)
British scientist

CAN I CHANGE THE PAST?

Some people believe in *fate*—the idea that everything is supposed to happen in a certain way. "It wasn't meant to be," they'll tell you, or "This is your destiny!" But you make choices all the time, so surely you're the one in charge of your life. Or do you just *think* you are?

And could you change things that have already happened to you? It's unlikely, but if scientists ever invent a time machine and you sneak your way onboard, perhaps you could go back and alter decisions you've made in the past. Imagine how a little change might have a big effect. Would you change the person you are now, or would you just change the person you were in the past? Hmmm. . . it all gets very difficult to figure out!

WHAT IS EMPTY SPACE IF IT'S NOT EMPTY?

Scientists know that even the remotest areas of outer space between stars are sprinkled with hydrogen atoms. But there's a lot more, too. Four percent of the universe is stuff we can see—everything here on Earth, stars, planets, and galaxies—but as for the other 96 percent. . . well, who knows?

The best bet is that most of the missing stuff is a mixture of dark matter and dark energy. This mysterious "darkness" can't be seen with telescopes, making it tough to figure out what it actually is.

Maybe the everyday things around you aren't normal. Earth, stars, planets, and galaxies are the odd ones out in a universe mostly made of dark matter and dark energy—stuff we can't capture, see, or explain. Not yet, anyway!

CAN WE SEE THE EDGE OF THE UNIVERSE?

Telescopes have been getting bigger and better since they were first used in the early 1600s.

In the 1920s, American scientist Edwin Hubble used a telescope to show that the universe contained more galaxies than just our Milky Way. The Hubble Space Telescope named after him has orbited Earth for more than 20 years, sending back images of distant galaxies and allowing scientists to estimate the age of the universe.

Telescopes have shown us how huge the universe is and what some of it looks like. Will we reach a limit on how far we can see, or will we one day spot the very edge of the universe? That is, if the universe *has* an edge. . .

WHERE ARE ALL THE ALIENS?

Scientists sometimes call Earth a "Goldilocks" planet. Like Baby Bear's porridge in the fairy tale, it isn't too hot or too cold—it's just right! But are there other Goldilocks planets? Our galaxy alone (there are billions and billions more) has up to 400 billion stars. Some of these must be orbited by planets like ours with liquid water—something needed for life as we know it.

American astronomer Frank Drake came up with a formula to predict how many advanced life forms might exist in our galaxy. After a lot of number crunching, he said there may be 10,000 civilizations out there. Scientists have been listening for messages from space since the 1960s, but they have received no response. If the universe is crawling with aliens, why don't they reply?

IS SCIENCE A

Science is about discovery. Modern science is a process of looking at things, coming up with ideas, testing them, and trying to find *evidence*—proof—of things using experiments. Some might say it's the search for *truth*.

To figure out whether science is a good thing or not, maybe we first need to decide what the point of it is. Is discovering new things supposed to make us happier? Should it make our lives easier and healthier? Or should science just keep our big brains from getting bored?

Science has found things that seem to improve our world, from new medicines to weather forecasting.

GOOD THING?

But it's also brought trouble in the form of dangerous weapons and energy-guzzling machines that pollute our planet. So can we ever say whether science is completely good or completely bad?

One of the most amazing scientists of all time, Albert Einstein, once said, "The important thing is not to stop questioning." There is a lot left for us to learn. Will we ever know everything? Will the world be a better place if we do? What do *you* think?

GLOSSARY

Words in **bold** refer to other glossary entries.

ALIEN Forms of life that we think might exist on other planets.

AMINO ACID Compounds in the body making up the "building blocks" of proteins.

ANESTHETIC A **chemical** used to stop people from feeling sensations, including pain. General anesthetic makes a patient go to sleep.

ANCESTORS People that were alive a very long time ago and are related to humans living today. Your great-great-grandparents are recent ancestors of yours, but it goes back much further than that!

ASTRONOMER A scientist who learns about space and the **universe** beyond Earth.

ATMOSPHERE The layers of gases surrounding Earth and vital for life. The atmosphere keeps our planet warm by trapping the Sun's heat inside—this is called the "greenhouse effect."

ATOM A basic unit of matter. The word *atom* comes from the Greek word *atomos*, which means "uncuttable."

BACTERIA Tiny **organisms** made of a single cell, some of which can cause diseases, such as cholera.

BIG BANG A huge explosion that created the **universe** 13.7 billion years ago.

BLACK HOLE A region of space from which nothing, not even light, can escape.

BRAIN The organ inside the skull at the center of the nervous system, controlling everything you think and do.

CELL The smallest unit of a living thing. Each cell is so small that it can usually only be seen under a powerful microscope.

CHEMICAL A particular substance, often something made in a laboratory by a chemist.

CLONE An identical copy of a living thing. Clones share exactly the same **DNA**.

DARK ENERGY A supposed form of energy that is spread through all of space and tends to increase the rate that the **universe** is expanding.

DARK MATTER An invisible form of matter that is thought to make up most of the **universe**.

DINOSAURS Extinct creatures that inhabited Earth from 201 million years ago to 66 million years ago.

DNA A **chemical** that forms the basic "building blocks" of living things, carrying genetic information. DNA is short for deoxyribonucleic acid.

ELECTRICITY A form of energy coming from charged particles, such as electrons gathering together or flowing in one direction. Lightning is a type of electricity.

ELECTRON A particle that is part of all atoms. Electrons have a negative charge.

EMOTION A strong feeling that affects your body, expression, thoughts, and behavior. Most people experience the main emotions—such as anger, fear, and happiness—in similar ways.

EVIDENCE Facts that support a theory, making it more likely to be true.

EVOLUTION The process by which living things change and develop over long periods of time.

EXTINCTION The end of a **species**, usually when the last individual is known to have died.

FOOD CHAIN The links made between animals and plants according to what they eat. For example, a seagull eats big fish, which eat little fish, which eat shrimp, which eat plankton.

FORMULA A shorthand way of explaining information with symbols, often used in math and chemistry. A formula can also mean a specific mixture of **atoms** and **molecules**.

GALAXY A massive collection of **stars**, gas, and dust bound together by **gravity** in one system. The galaxy we live in is called the Milky Way.

GAS A state of matter in which particles are spread far apart and can fill up any space. Air is made up of many different **gases**, such as oxygen and nitrogen.

GENE A section of **DNA**. Most genes store the code for a particular protein.

GRAVITY A natural phenomenon by which things attract each other. Gravity is responsible for keeping Earth in orbit around the Sun.

HALLUCINATION An experience during which someone sees or hears something that isn't really there.

INFINITE Something that appears to have no limits in size, time, or space. It continues forever.

INVENTION A new machine, product, or way of doing things that is different from anything before.

MICROSCOPIC Something so small that it is visible only through a microscope.

MOLECULE A group of two or more **atoms** held together by **chemical** bonds.

NEURON A **cell** that can send and receive messages with electrical and chemical signals. Neurons make up the nervous system in the body, including the **brain** and the spinal cord.

ORGANIC A substance coming from a living or dead **organism**.

ORGANISM
Any living thing.

PHILOSOPHER
Someone who tries to solve problems by thinking about how we look at the world around us.

PHOTOSYNTHESIS
The process by which green plants and some other **organisms** turn sunlight into chemical energy.

PSYCHOLOGIST
A type of medical specialist who researches why the **brain** makes us behave in certain ways. It is the job of some psychologists to help people deal with behavioral problems caused by their brains.

SOLAR SYSTEM
The Sun and all the other bodies bound to it by **gravity**, including planets, asteroids, and comets.

SPECIES
A group of similar living things that can breed together and produce offspring. Humans are an example of a species.

STAR
A great ball of **gas** held together by its own gravity. The Sun is a star.

TELESCOPE
An instrument designed to make distant objects appear closer by focusing light through a series of lenses and mirrors. We use telescopes to study space.

UNIVERSE
Everything that exists, all of space and time, and all the matter and energy within it.

VACCINE
A medicine that helps prevent someone from catching a particular disease.

VIRUS
A tiny thing that can only replicate (copy itself) inside other living **cells**. Some viruses cause diseases.

INDEX

FURTHER READING

BOOKS

Really, Really Big Questions about Life, the Universe and Everything by Dr. Stephen Law

Really, Really Big Questions about Space and Time by Mark Brake

Really, Really Big Questions about Me by Dr. Stephen Law

Supergeek! Robots, Space and Furry Animals by Glenn Murphy

WEBSITES

Science news:
www.eurekalert.org/kidsnews/

Games:
http://kids.usa.gov/teens-home/play-games/science/index.shtml

Experiments and articles:
www.planet-science.com/

THINKING LIKE A SCIENTIST

Here are some top tips to get your brain thinking just like a scientist:

1. Get out and about to see as much as you can—ideas are everywhere! Try museums, parks, zoos, and events going on in your local area.

2. Don't be afraid to guess. All scientists make guesses about what they think the answer will be before testing it out for themselves.

3. Ask other people what they think. It might help to test your questions and, to spark new ideas. Two heads are better than one!

4. Remember that you don't have to understand everything. It's okay to ask for help or explanations.

5. Never stop asking questions. . .

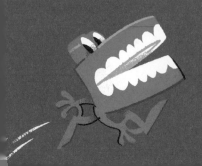